ARE CUSTOMERS BEING SERVED?

How to boost profits by delivering exceptional customer service

An Easy Step by Step Guide

BY

PAULINE ROWSON

Published by Rowmark Limited
65 Rogers Mead
Hayling Island
Hampshire
PO11 0PL

ISBN: 978-0-9548045-5-8
First published in 2006
Copyright © Pauline Rowson 2006

The right of Pauline Rowson to be identified as the author of this work has been asserted by her in accordance with the Copyright, Design and Patents Act 1988.

All rights reserved. No part of this publication may be reproduced in any material form (including photocopying or storing it in any medium by electronic means and whether or not transiently or incidentally to some other use of publication) without the written permission of the copyright owner except in accordance with the provisions of the Copyright, Designs and Patents Act 1988 or under the terms of a licence issued by the Copyright Licensing Agency Ltd. 90 Tottenham Court Road, London, England W1P 9HE. Applications for the copyright owner's written permission to reproduce any part of this publication should be addressed to the publisher.

Warning: The doing of an unauthorised act in relation to a copyright work may result in both a civil claim for damages and criminal prosecution.

Note: The material contained in this book is set out in good faith for general guidance and no liability can be accepted for loss or expense incurred as a result of relying in particular circumstances on statements made in this book.

Other *Easy Step by Step Guides*:

Sales and Marketing Books

Telemarketing, Cold Calling & Appointment Making

Marketing

Successful Selling

Building a Positive Media Profile

Writing Advertising Copy

Writing Articles and Newsletters

Personal Development Books

Stress and Time Management

Communicating with more Confidence

Giving Confident Presentations

Being Positive and Staying Positive even when the going gets Tough

Management Books

Motivating your Staff

Recruiting the Right Staff

Better Budgeting for your Business

Managing Change

Handling Confrontation

Writing a Business Plan and Making it Work

Negotiating for Success

Other books in the series

Publishing and Promoting your Book
Fundraising for your School

All the above guides are available from bookshops and on line, and as ebooks.

Rowmark Limited
E mail: enquiries@rowmark.co.uk
www.rowmark.co.uk

Books by Pauline Rowson

Crime Fiction – Marine Mysteries

In Cold Daylight

Tide of Death

In for the Kill

Non-fiction

Communicating with more Confidence

Being Positive and Staying Positive even when the going gets Tough

Marketing

Successful Selling

Telemarketing, Cold Calling & Appointment Making

Building a Positive Media Profile

Fundraising for your School

Publishing and Promoting your Book

Pauline Rowson

PAULINE ROWSON lives in the UK and has helped countless organizations to improve their customer service skills. She is author of several marketing and self-help books and for many years ran her own successful marketing, PR and training company. She is a popular speaker at conferences and workshops and is also the author of the popular marine mystery series of crime and thriller novels.

Praise for The Easy Step by Step Guides

Recruiting the Right Staff
'A simple guide to recruitment, with checklists of how and where to advertise job vacancies, whether to use agencies or not, and how to devise an ideal candidate profile. Perfect for step-by-step essentials.'
Management Today

Telemarketing, Cold Calling & Appointment Making
'This book is highly informative, clearly written and covers every aspect of telemarketing. In fact, it contains everything you need to know about how to build your business by telephone.'
HSBC Bank

What our readers say about a variety of our Easy Step by Step Guides

'Highly informative, very interesting, extremely practical and down to earth advice.'

'Excellent – no fancy jargon just plain simple facts.'

'Lots of good info, easy to read and concise. Very useful.'

'Each chapter is presented with a clear type face, lots of bullet points summarising previous text and some information boxed making the whole very easy to read.'

'I particularly like the boxes containing key statements and the easy to read and digest summaries – ideal for the busy person.'

'Clear, reader friendly and full of helpful hints.'

'I refer to my copy often and have found the summary sections and the highlighted hints invaluable.'

'A most practical, helpful guide.'

Easy Step by Step Guides

- Quick and easy to read – from cover to cover in two hours

- Contain a handy bullet point summary at the end of each chapter

- Provide lots of tips and techniques

- Have a simple style and layout – making the books easy to read

- Jargon free – straightforward and easy to understand

- Written by practitioners – people with experience and who are 'experts' in their subject.

Contents

Chapter 3
Building a competitive advantage 39

Chapter 4
Developing a customer service policy 51

Chapter 7

Assertiveness **85**

Chapter 8

Dealing with the angry or difficult person 95

Chapter 9

Chapter 10

Introduction

How often have you heard remarks like this?

You're the fifth person to complain about that today!

Everyone moans about that?

We can't *possibly* do *that*?

If it's not on the shelf we haven't got it.

I'll put you on hold…

Sound familiar? I expect you've got many more examples of poor customer service. And this doesn't only apply to shops but to all types of businesses: from solicitors to IT companies, from the public sector to the medical profession, plumbers, builders, banks, butchers and candlestick makers. If you're in business you have customers, whether they are called patients, clients, passengers they are all CUSTOMERS. They hand over their money to you in exchange for a product or a service.

You are my customer. You have parted with your money and purchased this book. You have certain expectations from this book. If it disappoints you, then you become a dissatisfied customer, and you may not purchase other books in The Easy Step by Step Guide series.

Where did you purchase this book? Was it in on the Internet or in a bookshop? What was the service like? Will you buy a book from that organization again? If not, why not?

Having a good reputation for excellent service and products is one very successful way of building a competitive advantage for your business. But be warned, a good reputation is not easy to attain, or retain. This book will show you how to do both.

How to use this guide

This guide is written in as clear a style as possible to help you. I recommend that you read it through from beginning to end and then dip into it to refresh your memory. The boxes in each chapter contain tips to help you. Also at the end of each chapter is a handy summary of the points covered.

What you will learn

This guide will show you:

O How good customer relations can help you win more business

O How to win more business by retaining customers and gaining recommendations from them

O How to satisfy your customers' needs

O How to develop an effective customer service policy

O How to use positive behaviour and attitude to win more business

O How to build a better rapport with your customers

O How to handle anger, complaints and difficult customers and turn them into satisfied customers.

Chapter 1

Why do we need to provide good customer service?

Marketing strategies within organizations are often geared towards winning new business from new customers. This is all very well but what about winning more business from your existing customers?

Many organizations fail to realize the value of their existing customers, or the fact that they can sell more to them. They treat them in a cavalier manner, often ignoring them once the business is won, and in some cases making it as difficult as possible for customers to purchase products or services. It sometimes amazes me that businesses make any money at all. Of course some don't and subsequently fail. Many organizations chase the Holy Grail of obtaining new customers, spending time, money and energy on capturing them only to provide them with a service or product that quite frankly is inferior. What a waste.

If we do not look after our customers then someone else will. In addition, those dissatisfied customers will tell others about their awful experience with you. Once you have a negative reputation it is extremely difficult to reverse.

As a general rule the following applies:

❑ 96% of dissatisfied customers do not go back and complain

❑ But they do tell 7 other people how bad you are

❑ 13% will tell at least 20 others

❑ 90% will never return

❑ It probably costs 8 times as much to attract a new customer as it does to keep an existing one

With those kind of figures isn't it foolish not to get things right inside your organization?

So what goes wrong?

There are several things that can and do go wrong within an organization. Just think for a moment of all the things that annoy you when you are a customer. Draw up a list. Now look at my list below, is it very similar to yours, or do you have some additional points?

○ Being passed around

○ People not returning calls

○ Having to chase up all the time

○ People not taking ownership of the problem

○ Obvious insincerity

○ Poor communication of mistakes and problems

○ Being kept waiting

○ Voice mail and music whilst on hold and the telephonist never coming back to you

○ Staff not knowing enough about who does what

○ Staff making mistakes – again and again

O Arrogance and complacency

O Rigid inflexible procedures

O Being patronized

O Staff who couldn't care less/are rude/lacking in product knowledge

O Not delivering on time!

And sadly there are many more...

The question you need to ask yourself is how sure are you that these things aren't happening in your organization?

Providing good customer service is essential for the survival and success of your business. It is not just about smiling at the customer and saying, 'Have a nice day,' but, as you will see from this book, it goes much deeper. Providing excellent customer service is a philosophy, a complete way of doing business. Delivering exceptional customer service is a complex, onerous and never ending task, but its rewards can be huge in terms of job satisfaction, motivated staff and increased profits.

How to get more business from your existing customers

By getting your customers to climb on board **the loyalty ladder** you can increase sales for your organization.

Satisfied customers become - advocates

Satisfied customers become - repeat purchasers

Satisfied customers bring you - prospects

Who in turn become customers.

Word of mouth recommendation is a very powerful and highly cost effective marketing tool.

Providing excellent customer service **consistently** is not easy, far from it. Why? Because **people** deliver customer services, **people** make products and provide a service, and **people** are fallible.

We all have different personalities, varying degrees of confidence, and diverse styles of communication. We have good days and bad days. We have moods, headaches and heartaches, and all these effect how we perform and interact with others. Is it no wonder that we can sometimes get it wrong!

Your challenge as a manager, director or owner of an organization is to minimize these problems, eliminate the scope for error, and provide guidelines and rules to help people perform in a manner that will satisfy your customers. Above all *you* need **to set an example** (even when *you* have a headache!)

**Good customer service
starts at the TOP.**

And if you're still not convinced that providing good customer service is essential to your business here are twelve more reasons why you should take the time to get this right.

Twelve benefits of providing good customer service

1. Increased revenue

2. Increased efficiency

3. Less waste

4. Improved staff morale and confidence

5. Reduction in staff turnover and absenteeism

6. Saves money

7. Enables individuals to take responsibility – saves time

8. Increased customer confidence – which leads to more purchases

9. Gives employees a sense of pride in the company – increased motivation

10. Increased profits

11. Happier shareholders (if you have them)

12. Less bad publicity, more good publicity, which in turn brings in more customers.

Plus there is another overwhelming and compelling reason for providing excellent customer service – it can give you an edge on your competitors.

In order to provide this, you and your staff need to develop good interpersonal skills, which means you need to be able to:

○ Listen and interpret needs accurately
○ Ask the right questions
○ Have a positive attitude
○ Be tactful and helpful
○ Have an open mind about people
○ Have good self esteem
○ Be quick thinking
○ Have an assertive manner
○ Be approachable and well mannered
○ Have excellent communication skills
○ Be a good team player
○ Have good body language and a presentable appearance

You also need to understand three vital things:

1. **Who your customers are**
2. **What they want from you**
3. **Why they buy from you**

The following chapters will help you to:

○ Analyze your market

○ Draw up a customer service policy

○ Provide you with some interpersonal skills to help deliver that excellent customer service.

In summary

○ if you don't look after your customers then someone else will

○ dissatisfied customers will tell others about their awful experience with you

○ once you have a negative reputation it is extremely difficult to reverse it

○ providing good customer service is essential for the survival and success of your business

○ delivering exceptional customer service can reap rewards in terms of job satisfaction, motivated staff and increased profits

○ satisfied customers become advocates, repeat purchasers and recommend you to others

○ excellent customer service can give you an edge on your competitors

○ you and your staff need to develop good interpersonal skills

○ you also need to understand three vital things:

Who your customers are
What they want from you
Why they buy from you

Chapter 2

Who are your customers?

The more you know about your customers the more successful you will be in delivering to them the kind of exceptional service they require. But this isn't as straightforward as it seems because you may have many different groups of customers all with different needs.

Let's take the example of a local newspaper, its customers are:

- O Readers
- O Advertisers
- O Shareholders
- O Councils and other local organizations
- O Newsagents
- O Regulatory bodies
- O Suppliers
- O Staff

Although there may be some overlap, each group of customers will require different things from you in order to become a satisfied customer. Readers want a lively, entertaining and informative newspaper, whereas advertisers want increased profile for their organizations and more customers. Councils may wish to inform and educate; shareholders require a profitable newspaper; suppliers a healthy relationship with their customer and to be paid on time; and the staff want to work for a successful and interesting company.

You may be surprised that I have included both suppliers and staff on the above list. Although strictly speaking neither are customers, each group, however, forms an impression of the organization and that impression is communicated to the outside world. If suppliers say it is difficult to get paid by the organization for the services or products they have supplied, this may well spread a rumour that the organization is in financial difficulty, or that they are awkward to deal with. This message can have a negative impact in the market place.

Likewise with staff, if they say negative things about the organization they work for then word is likely to get around. Not only will the organization find it difficult to recruit highly motivated and good quality staff but they will also find that this negative message spreads to their customer base and therefore affects the organization's reputation.

Suppliers and staff are potential customers too, and they have a part to play in communicating your reputation whether for good or bad to your market place.

> **Look carefully at your customer base.**
> **Be precise about who your**
> **customers are and what markets**
> **you are serving.**

What do your customers want?

When people buy a product or service they also consider the emotional factors that surround that purchase. For example when a woman buys a hair cut, it is not just the quality of the cut and the style, but she will also take into consideration the attitude of the hairstylist and other staff; whether she is welcomed and feels comfortable, and the reputation of that salon. In a restaurant you are considering not only the quality and quantity of food but also the atmosphere of the restaurant, its décor, the other clientele, the cleanliness and facilities of the restaurant, its location and accessibility.

Let's see what our groups of customers want from our newspaper example.

Readers

The readers' want:

> Information
> Entertainment
> A relationship with the newspaper
> Quality
> Accuracy
> Reputation
> An affinity with the newspaper
> To be educated
> Value for money
> Continuity
> Professionalism
> Empathy

Advertisers

The advertisers want:

> Customers
> Job applicants
> A relationship with the newspaper and its staff
> Quality
> Accuracy
> Reputation
> Brand
> Value for money
> Security/reliability
> Results
> Continuity
> Professionalism
> Empathy
> Service

Staff

The staff want:

> Job satisfaction
> Enjoyment
> A career
> A salary package
> Security
> Relationships
> Good feedback

Praise
Constructive criticism
Recognition
Professionalism
Training/development
Pride
Commitment
Effective management
A positive company image
Responsibility
Purpose
Colleagues
Leadership
Communication
Loyalty

And to cap it all, different members of staff will want varying degrees of the above. Your task as a manager (or owner/director) is to find out what motivates that particular staff member and then deliver it. (For more information on motivating staff see our sister publication *The Easy Step by Step Guide to Motivating Your Staff for Better Performance*.)

By understanding and delivering these emotional factors to your customers, and satisfying them consistently, you will excel in providing customer service and gain a competitive advantage.

Now take a look at *your* customer list and put the emotional factors beside each group of customers. Then ask yourself if your organization is delivering this.

Why do your customers buy?

Having looked at **what** customers buy, let's now examine **why** they buy.

People generally buy for two reasons:

- O Objective
- O Subjective

In order to deliver good customer service you will need to satisfy both of these.

Objective reasons

These are often associated with a physiological need. For example, you might buy a meal in a restaurant or café to satisfy a basic **physiological need** in that you are hungry. You dive into the first café you come to, or the only restaurant that has vacant spaces. A need to satisfy your hunger pang is the **objective reason** for buying.

In another example you might require the services of a solicitor, perhaps for a divorce, or to draw up a contract. You need to comply with the law. That is the **objective reason** for buying.

Now let's look at the subjective reasons.

Subjective reasons

Although you are hungry you might still ask yourself a series of questions before diving into the nearest café. For example: does it look like my sort of place? Who are the clientele and will I feel comfortable with them? Is the café clean? Does the restaurant have the right choice of food and beverages for me?

These are the **subjective reasons**. They are based on your personal preferences and are referred to as the **psychological reasons** involved in making a buying decision. Often, as we discussed previously, they are the emotional factors surrounding a purchase.

In respect of our legal firm example, you might be asking yourself the following questions before choosing a particular lawyer or legal firm:

○ does the lawyer understand my situation?

○ does the lawyer have the technical expertise to deal with my problem?

○ does he/she talk my language?

○ does the law firm provide an efficient service?

○ what is its reputation?

○ how am I treated when I telephone or visit them?

○ how responsive are they to my requests and demands?

○ do they have the depth of specialist knowledge?

○ what is the cost and can I afford it?

○ can I relate to my lawyer?

The legal firm must make sure it delivers on all the above. If it fails to live up to expectations then the customer (or client) will be dissatisfied with the service, and might also tell others, thereby damaging future business for the firm.

In summary

O different groups of customers have different needs

O the more you know about your customers the more successful you will be in delivering to them the kind of exceptional service/ products they require

O suppliers and staff form an impression of the organization and that impression is communicated to the outside world, make sure it isn't a negative one

O when people buy a product or service they also consider the emotional factors that surround that purchase

O by understanding and delivering these emotional factors to your customers, and satisfying them consistently, you will excel in providing customer service and gain a competitive advantage

O People generally buy for two reasons:

  O   Objective
  O   Subjective

○ In order to deliver good customer service you will need to satisfy both of these

○ **Objective reasons** are often associated with a physiological need

○ **Subjective reasons** are referred to as the psychological reasons involved in making a purchase.

Chapter 3

Building a competitive advantage

I have already mentioned that providing excellent customer service is a way of building a competitive advantage for your organization. In addition, having a clearly defined image of what your organization stands for, consistently communicating it, and living up to that image is what it also takes to stand out from the crowd. So let's take a closer look at this.

Image

You never get a second chance to make a first impression and neither does your organization.

First impressions are often lasting impressions and could lose you vital business if they are negative ones. How many times have you walked out of a restaurant or hotel because you didn't like the look of the place? How many times have you telephoned an organization to make an enquiry, to place an order, or make a booking and changed your mind because you were kept hanging on the telephone, or were passed from person to person, or found the member of staff on the other end of the line off hand and unhelpful? Exactly! I hope it doesn't happen in your organization, but you'd better check, just in case...

It is very easy to get blasé about your own organization; after all, you work there, and therefore see it day in and day out, and because of this you eventually stop seeing it. It becomes wallpaper. You are too busy worrying about that next order, or that report, or what your boss thinks about you, or your personal problems to notice your surroundings. You don't see that things aren't how they should be. It often takes an outsider to point out the blindingly obvious.

So step back and take a good, long, hard look at your organization from the prospective customer's point of view. Here is a questionnaire to help you. It can be adapted depending on your type of organization.

Assess your organization - Is it giving out the correct impression?

Rate your organization on a scale of 0-5 (5 = high, 0 = low)

❑ Location of the business

Are you easily accessible to your customers and suppliers (Do you need to be)?

❑ Building outside

What does it look like? Is it clean? Is the signage clear and creating the right image for your organization? Is the entrance clearly marked? Is there car parking for visitors? Is this clearly displayed?

❑ Building inside

Is the reception area clean, fresh and tidy? Are the public areas clean, and tidy? Is the paintwork good? Is the furniture comfortable? Are there paintings on the walls? Is the company sign clearly displayed? Are there magazines or company brochures available for your customers to read? Have you used the space to promote your products/services? Are the interview or meeting rooms clean, tidy and comfortable? What kind of image do you want to give out in your conference or boardroom? Is this being achieved? Are the visitor toilets clean and well equipped?

❑ Reception and front line staff

The receptionist – is he/she smartly dressed or in uniform provided? Is he/she clean and presentable? Does he/she smile on greeting the customer? Does the receptionist get the customer's name and use it? Does the receptionist invite the customer to take a seat? Does he/she offer the customer a coffee or tea? (If appropriate). If there is a delay does the receptionist keep the customer informed?

The receptionist is often the first person in an organization to come into contact with the customer. It is vitally important, therefore, that you have the right person for this job. This also applies to all those employees who are front line staff.

Why is it that some companies put the dragon on reception, or that some organizations seem to recruit and place in the front line the most unhelpful individuals they can find? Is it because nobody else wants to work with them? Or is it because you have recruited in a hurry, or because you are not very good at interviewing and appointing staff? Taking time to get this right could save you a great deal of time in the future not to mention money. (For more information on recruiting and appointment staff see *The Easy Step by Step Guide to Recruiting the Right Staff*.)

Also ensure that your reception and public areas do not become gossip zones. I have overheard staff grumbling about their company and the individuals within the company on many occasions. It is highly unprofessional and creates a very negative opinion in the mind of the customer.

Answering the telephone

The telephone may be the first point of contact for the customer within your organization. Indeed in some cases it may be the only point of contact.

❏ How is the telephone answered?

Do you have a policy that it is answered within five rings, or do all your staff leave their telephones on voice mail and **never** return calls? Is this appropriate behaviour for an organization that promotes itself as being customer friendly? I don't think so!

How often do your customers get passed around between departments? If you have an automated call system is it helpful and appropriate? Most people hate them, but sadly they are a fact of life. Is it important to your organization for the customer to speak to a real person rather than press buttons and feed information into a telephone keypad? If you are providing a product or service to an elderly group of customers then personal contact will be extremely important to them, and the pressing of buttons in an automated call system highly inappropriate.

❑ Staff behaviour and attitude

When your staff speak to the customer what is their manner like? Those who are abrupt, impatient and can only speak in monosyllables are not what you need. Neither are individuals who chatter away endlessly. If you have staff who are handling complaints then they need to know how to do this professionally. (See chapter eight for more on this.)

How do your staff behave towards your customers? How should they address them – by their surname or first name? How should they respond to customer enquiries? What is the length of time they should take to respond to enquiries by telephone or letter? Do you have a policy to state this and if so is it monitored regularly to see if it is being delivered?

Dealing with the public is highly demanding and requires excellent interpersonal skills. Not everyone is equipped to do the job. Make sure you recruit those individuals who can and indeed who enjoy serving the public. In addition, provide them with ongoing training and refresher skills.

❏ How are customer complaints handled?

Do you have a policy clarifying this? Do all the staff adhere to it? Are complaints systematically monitored and discussed? If something is wrong within your organization, do you take action to put it right?

The workplace environment

If a company doesn't care for the workplace environment and the well-being of its staff, then why should the staff care for the company? And if they don't care for the company then they won't care for the customers.

Staff areas

❏ Work stations – are these comfortable, functional and adequate for the task?

❑ Rest room/canteen – is there somewhere for the staff to relax when off duty, or to eat their lunch? Is this clean, tidy and well equipped?

❑ Toilets – are there adequate toilet facilities? Are they cleaned regularly?

❑ Equipment – do staff have the right equipment for the job? Inadequate and frequently failing equipment is often a demotivating factor and causes unnecessary delays and therefore lost profits.

So how did your organization score? Are there any areas that you need to look at and correct? Make a list of them, and draw up a timetable and budget to implement. Before you do this though you might like to ask your customers, staff and other visitors for their views and requirements. These might differ from your view because sometimes it is hard to be objective. But being objective is paramount if you wish to project the right image to your customers.

Know your products/services

In order to provide good customer service you need to have knowledgeable staff. This means providing ongoing product training for them. It is amazing how many organizations throw their staff in at the deep end with little or no product training and just expect them to 'pick it up as they go.' They may well do this, but how many customers have you alienated in the process, and how many sales have you lost?

Making sure the messages don't get mixed

Organizations often spend vast amounts of money in getting their external message right and fail to do the same inside the company. If you are telling your customers that you are a progressive organization, approachable, professional and reliable and yet when customers approach you they get a sloppy service, the premises are shabby and nobody ever returns their calls, then the customer will be gravely disappointed and will take their business elsewhere.

Be consistent

In order to deliver excellent customer service your message has to be consistent both inside and outside the organization. It is not merely a cosmetic exercise, though sadly many organizations think it is. You have to live the message.

Building a reputation

Building a reputation for excellence takes a considerable amount of time, destroying it can take seconds. By constantly checking the above factors you can begin to build a clearly defined image and reputation for your organization.

In summary

O having a clearly defined image of what your organization stands for, consistently communicating it and living up to that image is what it takes to stand out from the crowd

O you never get a second chance to make a first impression and neither does your organization

○ first impressions are often lasting impressions and could lose you vital business if they are negative.

○ take a long, hard look at your organization from the prospective customer's viewpoint, is it giving out the right impression?

○ are the staff giving out the right impression?

○ ask your customers, staff and other visitors for their views

○ make sure your front line staff are fully trained and able and willing to deal with the customer effectively and efficiently

○ ensure you have a policy that says how the telephone should be answered and how calls should be handled

○ ensure you have a policy that states how customer complaints should be handled

○ if something is wrong within your organization take action to put it right

○ dealing with the public is highly demanding and requires excellent interpersonal skills

○ if an organization doesn't care for the workplace environment and the well-being of its staff, then the staff won't care for the organization

○ in order to provide good customer service you need to have knowledgeable and well-trained staff

○ be consistent in your messages both inside and outside the organization

○ building a reputation for excellence takes a considerable amount of time, destroying it can take seconds.

Chapter 4

Developing a customer service policy

With people therefore being the key to developing the right impression of your organization, management must make it clear to individuals what is expected of them. To do this you need to have a clear policy. This policy will include the following:

○ A client orientated mission statement

○ Clear standards of what is expected

○ A strategy that communicates those standards

○ Ongoing staff training

○ A system to measure and monitor performance

○ A way of rewarding staff

○ A policy of providing continuing client care

Eight steps to building a customer service policy

STEP 1.

Developing a customer orientated mission

People need to know what the organization stands for so define its personality and its mission. To do this, ask your customers how they see you and how you can improve things. Ask your staff for their impressions and views and how you can improve things.

You might come up with a series of words that represent your organization like these below:

- O   Professional
- O   Progressive
- O   Friendly
- O   Trustworthy
- O   High quality
- O   Enthusiastic
- O   Approachable

These are fine words, but do they go far enough? They could apply to any company. Can you personalize these words to define your company more specifically?

Having defined it, you must live up to it otherwise your customers will be disappointed. Ensure that your staff believe in the mission statement and that they, and you, are committed to delivering it. Define excellence and make it your organization's objective

STEP 2.

Set standards

In order to provide excellent customer service your staff need to know what is expected of them. A written standard or code of practice can be very helpful. This can include standards for:

- behaviour
- dress/appearance
- delivery of your service
- quality of your product

Setting dress and behaviour codes can be highly contentious areas. In order to avoid dissent you need to involve your staff in drawing up these standards. This gives them ownership, which means they will be happier in complying with the rules once set. If you have a large organization it will be very difficult to involve everyone so setting up a small committee may be the answer. This committee can include a representative from each department who will take responsibility for obtaining feedback from team members, and reporting back any developments and outcomes to them. Once the policy is made and implemented ensure that all new staff are inducted in this.

Some organizations see no need to have a dress code. This is often dependent on the type of business and the customers that the business serves. Having a behaviour code may be a very different case. For example, you may wish to state that all telephone calls are to be answered within three to five rings; or that all customers are addressed formally. You may have other standards of behaviour that you expect from your staff, these can include punctuality, dealing with customer queries and complaints. All this can be contained within a behaviour or customer care code. Again, involve staff in drawing this up, and don't forget to induct new staff. Review this regularly, update and amend it. Measure and monitor performance against it and reward those staff who consistently deliver or exceed it.

STEP 3.

Communicate standards

Make it clear to staff what is expected of them and give them a real sense of personal responsibility. Develop an environment in which orders can be passed and carried out effectively. Ensure that your staff have a sense of belonging – making them feel simultaneously informed, involved and sharing in the success of the organization. Adhere to those standards yourself and encourage your staff to contribute new ideas /better ways of doing things.

A successful organization must be concerned with the personal wants, needs and desires of the individuals within its workforce. Communication is not just a case of slapping out a newsletter or bulletin, or holding meetings, but it involves actively inviting opinions, talking to individuals face-to-face and listening to them. Yes, it takes time, but it is essential to help your organization deliver that excellence in customer service. (For more on this see *The Easy Step by Step Guide to Motivating Your Staff for Better Performance.*)

STEP 4.

Train your staff

Give staff the training they need not only for their jobs but also in people skills. I examine people skills in chapters five to nine.

STEP 5.

Measure and monitor performance

You can do this through regular and valued performance reviews/appraisals. (See *The Easy Step by Step Guide to Motivating Your Staff for Better Performance* for more information on this.)

STEP 6.

Reward staff

Yes, it is nice to have a pay rise, and that is one way of rewarding staff, but there are other ways. Saying 'thank you' and giving genuine praise when it is deserved are two great means of rewarding and motivating people, and are often sadly lacking in organizations. They cost nothing but go a long way. You can also reward staff by promoting them, or perhaps assigning them to work on special projects.

STEP 7.

Plan for continuing and excellent customer service

Keep in touch with your customers and their views. Gain regular feedback from customers and staff. Alter the way you deliver a service if necessary and introduce new services or products that your customers are demanding.

STEP 8.

Good customer service starts with good recruitment

Ensure that you recruit the right people for the right job. Induct them fully; provide ongoing training and continually strive to improve internal communication. (See also *The Easy Step by Step Guide to Recruiting the Right Staff*).

The staff handbook

The staff handbook can be a valuable tool in ensuring your staff are aware of the organization's policies, mission and standards. Here are some guidelines on what the staff handbook might contain.

1. Introduction
About the organization
Its structure and background
Its mission statement

2. Conduct and discipline
Expected conduct
Behaviour, dress and other codes as required
Confidentiality
Disciplinary procedures
Grievance procedures

3. Salaries and benefits
Salaries
Pension schemes
Permanent health insurance
Private medical insurance
Public and Bank Holiday entitlement

4. Administrative procedures and rules

Standard working hours and timekeeping
Flexible working hours
Holiday rules
Sickness rules
Maternity policy
Compassionate leave
Allowances and expenses
Driving on firm's business
Eye testing for VDU's

5. Personnel policies and procedures

Induction
Training procedures
Staff appraisal procedures
Recruitment procedures
Statement of policy in accordance with the
Health & Safety at Work Acts
Policy on harassment
Equal opportunities policy

6. Client services policy

Clients' complaints procedures
Telephone answering policy

In summary

○ with people being the key to developing the right impression of your organization, management must make it clear to individuals what is expected of them

○ A customer service policy will include the following:

❏ A client orientated mission statement

❏ Clear standards of what is expected

❏ A strategy that communicates those standards

❏ On going staff training

❏ A system to measure and monitor performance

❏ A way of rewarding staff

❏ A policy of providing continuing customer care

○ involve your staff in drawing up policies, induct new staff, review policies regularly, update and amend them

○ measure and monitor staff performance, reward those members of staff who consistently deliver or exceed it

○ make it clear to staff what is expected of them and give them a real sense of personal responsibility

○ make sure staff have the training they need not only for them to carry out their jobs but also in people skills

○ the staff handbook can be a valuable tool in ensuring your staff are aware of the organization's policies, mission and standards.

Chapter 5

People skills

As I mentioned earlier, the people who deliver exceptional customer service need to have excellent interpersonal skills. These were listed in chapter one; here they are again:

You need to be able to:

- ○ Listen and interpret needs accurately
- ○ Ask the right questions
- ○ Have a positive attitude
- ○ Be tactful and helpful
- ○ Have an open mind about people
- ○ Have good self esteem
- ○ Be quick thinking
- ○ Have an assertive manner
- ○ Be approachable and well mannered
- ○ Have excellent communication skills
- ○ Be a good team player
- ○ Have good body language and a presentable appearance

It's quite a list! This and the following chapters cover the above points in more detail.

A presentable appearance and good body language

Staff who deal with customers, whether it be face-to-face or on the telephone, give out an impression of the organization. This impression is based on the following:

55% of the impression we make on other people is determined by what they SEE. This includes our colouring, appearance, posture, body language, facial expression, eye contact and handshake.

38% of the impression we make on others is determined by what they HEAR. How our voice sounds. Is it empathetic? Is it clear and assertive? Can the customer understand what we are saying? Do we have an accent? Rightly or wrongly we can be judged by our accent.

7% of the impression we make on others is determined by the WORDS they hear.

So how you look, react and sound is more important than the words you are using, certainly initially. Once the conversation develops this impression can, of course, change.

If the first and only impression you make is through the telephone then that whole area of what we see – 55% - moves into what we hear.

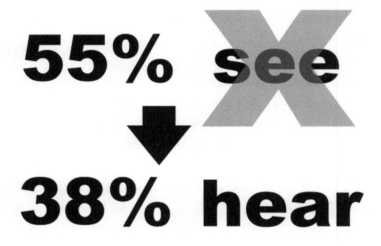

So that **93%** of the impression you give out is based on your voice.

If you, or your staff, work on the telephone handling customer queries and complaints, then how you sound is vitally important.

Appearance

How you look, your clothes and personal grooming and hygiene all play a part in creating an impression not only of you, but also of your organization. If you look dishevelled then people will think your organization is shoddy. If you look sloppy then the impression of your organization will be one of inefficiency. There is a vast choice when it comes to deciding what to wear and unfortunately some people lack dress sense and can wear inappropriate clothing in the workplace without even realising it. This is why many customer facing staff have a uniform. It reduces the room for error, and it presents a corporate image, one that the organization wishes to communicate to its customers. Uniforms can also be worn for practical reasons – nurses for example wear a uniform not only so that the patients can easily identify them but also because it can often be a messy job, and it saves them getting their own clothes dirty. Uniforms can take the worry out of deciding what to wear to work. They can also save the wearer money.

When it comes to deciding what to wear to work, women tend to make more mistakes than men because they have more choice: trousers, jeans, shorts, skirts, dresses, jumpers, T shirts, low cut tops, the list is endless, whereas men are more limited in their choice. That doesn't mean to say they don't make mistakes. We have all seen sloppily and inappropriately dressed men at work as well as women.

In some industries there is no dress code. That is fine as long as the individual who has to face the customer is clean and presentable.

If a staff member has a problem with hygiene then this must be dealt with tactfully. Rather than telling someone that their hair looks awful, and they should go home and wash it, perhaps on a day when they have washed it you could compliment them!

If you don't deal with a delicate situation, like a hygiene, or dress problem, as soon as it arises, then it will only make you feel awkward and even resentful towards that staff member. This will show in your body language and behaviour, and in turn make that individual surly and resentful.

Body piercing and tattoos can be another thorny topic. If you have clearly stated your policy on this at an interview, and it is written in the staff handbook, which the staff member has seen, and he/she has received a proper induction, then there shouldn't be a problem with this.

Body language

How you project yourself through your body language is vitally important. You may be speaking the right words, but if your body language is communicating a different message then it is that message that your recipient/s will react to.

Non-verbal signals are said to be at least four and a half times as effective as verbal signals and facial expressions eight times as powerful as the words used. We look at someone a third of the time we are talking to them and this look can convey anything from boredom and irritation to enthusiasm and liking. If you are in a situation where you are annoyed with (or don't like) the customer in front of you then your body language could betray your emotions. You could start to fidget, look bored, avoid eye contact, glance at your watch, all this will only serve to make that customer even more awkward or angry. Front line staff need to know how to control their emotions and the chapter on a positive inner voice will help them to do so.

> **You need to keep an open mind and open your mind about people.**

You can also enhance the image you project, and your feelings of self-confidence, by deliberately using more positive body language. Positive body language will send positive messages to your brain, which in turn will send even more positive messages back to your body language.

Positive body language

Positive messages to the brain

More positive body language

Customer reacts to positive body language from the member of staff

Greeting the customer

When greeting the customer the first impression is vitally important. The body language signals are:

○   the handshake
○   eye contact
○   the smile

Your handshake

Whether or not you shake hands with customers is dependent on your type of organization, the situation you are in and the sector in which you operate. If you, or your staff shake hands with customers then make sure the handshake is giving out the right impression. The handshake also creates a good opportunity to establish a rapport.

Your handshake can say a great deal about you. A firm dry handshake reveals confidence, professionalism and status. If you have a weak handshake it will convey the impression of a weak person, even if you aren't.

When you shake hands take the whole hand in a firm gip, not just the fingers. Be aware of the other person's handshake and if it is not as strong as yours then weaken yours a little to help build rapport. If it is stronger than yours, try not to wince. Just return the pressure slightly.

Always offer your hand first and invariably the other person will take it. Your elbow should be tucked into your waist when you shake hands and not outstretched. The handshake is a fairly universal greeting but if you are working with customers from different cultures please be aware that this might not be their normal form of greeting. A nod and smile should suffice.

What is your handshake like? Try shaking hands with someone you know and ask them for their honest opinion. If you need to firm it up then practice it.

Personal space

Personal space is the space around us that we feel comfortable in. We only allow those close to us to invade that space. If others do invade, uninvited, then we feel threatened by it and wish to step back. Make sure you are not invading your customers' personal space. Different cultures have different distances so be aware of this. British people are usually comfortable at a distance of about three feet.

Here are some more body language signals for you to be aware of.

Positive body language signals

O Try linking your hands together in front of you on the desk, as though to form a steeple, this can prevent you making nervous mannerisms. It also suggests confidence and self-possession.

O Stillness suggests ease and comfort in a situation, especially the ability to keep hands and feet still and relaxed. Don't fidget. Sit upright and alert. Give your customer good eye contact.

O Gestures showing open palms of hands demonstrate openness and confidence.

O Sitting asymmetrical demonstrates confidence and is less threatening to the other person than sitting face on, especially if it is across a table or desk.

O Leaning forward indicates interest, but don't move too close or you could be intimidating your customer by invading their personal space.

○ When standing, keep your hands and arms relaxed at your side. Don't fold your arms, it is a closed gesture and can look threatening and defensive.

○ If you need to take notes try not to do so constantly. Jot down key points and then give your customer (the speaker) regular eye contact.

○ Turn your body to the speaker/customer and look interested in what they are saying. Tell yourself that you *are* interested, as it will show on your expression. If you are thinking 'this person is boring the pants off me,' then your expression will reflect this.

○ When listening keep your body open, arms leaning forward on the table, hands gently folded. Relaxed.

Negative body language signals to avoid

○ Nervous mannerisms include nail biting, finger and foot tapping, playing with hair, or adjusting clothing, smoothing eyebrows

○ Playing with objects and personal effects; wedding rings, pencils etc. often indicates tension

○ Pointing at people, waving your fist, thumping the table, shows aggression and tension. Hopefully you won't be doing any of this, although your customer might be!

○ Touching the face is associated with negative emotions – guilt, self-doubt, and irritation. Likewise touching the chin and mouth shows doubt, a reluctance to speak or accept what is being said. Touching the nose is said to be an indication of lying; touching the eye not liking what you are seeing or not wanting to see any further, and touching the ears not liking what you are hearing.

Posture

Good posture is about the natural alignment of the head and spine with the body. It is governed by habit and can be difficult to change. The chin thrust forward is fairly typical of an aggressive, go-ahead personality. Someone who is deaf in one ear will listen extra hard with the other ear and will tilt their head forward. A short podgy person who habitually slumps will draw attention to his/her size. Fashions can affect posture – high heels, tight skirts. The body feels differently in different clothes and will affect your posture. Try to keep your posture upright, your shoulders back and your chin up (but not too high). Having a good posture will also help to send positive messages to your brain and will in turn make you feel more confident and self assured and able to deal with your customers in an assertive manner.

In summary

○ the people who deliver exceptional customer service need to have good interpersonal skills

○ staff who deal with customers give out an impression of your organization

○ 55% is based on what they SEE

○ 38% is based on what they HEAR

○ 7% is determined by the WORDS they hear

○ on the telephone the whole area of what we see – 55% moves into what we hear, so that **93%** is based on your voice

○ how you look plays an important part in creating an impression

○ how you project yourself through your body language is vitally important

○ non verbal signals are said to be at least four and a half times as effective as verbal signals and facial expressions eight times as powerful as the words used

○ we look at someone a third of the time we are talking to them and this look can convey anything from boredom and irritation to enthusiasm and liking

○ you can enhance the image you project and your feelings of self-confidence by deliberately using more positive body language

○ your handshake can say a great deal about you. A firm dry handshake reveals confidence, professionalism and status

○ personal space is the space around us that we feel comfortable with, don't threaten others by invading their personal space

○ try to keep your posture upright, your shoulders back and your chin up (but not too high)

Chapter 6

Listening

> **Listening, really listening is the
> hardest thing to do and the highest
> form of courtesy!**

We all think we listen well, but do we? Try this quick
questionnaire to find out how much you know about
listening. Simply answer true or false to the following
questions.

Questionnaire

1. Most people listen more than they speak
    ❑   True   ❑   False

2. Good listeners don't say anything while they listen
    ❑   True   ❑   False

3. Good listeners look at the speaker
    ❑   True   ❑   False

4. People listen well when they feel strongly about the topic
   ❑ True   ❑ False

5. Listeners are more influenced by what is said than how it is said
   ❑ True   ❑ False

6. People listen to criticism
   ❑ True   ❑ False

Answers:

1. **True** – yes there are more people who listen more than they speak, yet we all know those individuals who like the sound of their voice and never give anyone a chance of having their say. And, although we might listen, how much of that is quality listening, or how much simply drifts in one ear and out of the other?

2. **False** – good listeners give the listening noises when they listen e.g. uh huh, I see, really. This helps to confirm to the speaker that they are genuinely listening.

3. **True** – good listeners always look at the speaker.

4. **False** – people do not listen well when they feel strongly about a topic because their own feelings get in the way. They are just waiting for the speaker to finish so they can jump in and give their views.

5. **True** – Do you remember what I said earlier? 38% of the way we communicate is through our voice, how it sounds is often more important than what is being said.

6. **False** – we do not listen well to criticism because our personal feelings get in the way.

Listening is an essential part of being a good communicator and being good at delivering customer service. As more and more of our communication becomes visual and text driven, i.e. Internet, text, and computers we are forgetting how to listen. Listening involves both the ability to understand what is being said, and the ability to organize and analyze the messages in order to retain them for subsequent use.

There are two types of listening:

1. Casual listening
2. Critical listening

Casual listening

Casual listening is what we tend to do most of the time. We are only half listening, we retain bits of the conversation and we discard other parts of it. As a result you often get the following scenario between two people:

> 'Don't forget that order is due in today.'
> 'Is it? You didn't tell me.'
> 'Yes, I did, two days ago. You weren't listening.'

Critical listening

Critical listening requires concentration and stamina. Here you are making a real effort to understand the other person's point of view. You are listening to them, retaining what they say, storing it away and then retrieving some of it later when you need it. These skills are essential in a customer service situation.

So what stops us listening?

There are many things that prevent us from listening not least of which is laziness. We simply can't be bothered. Or maybe we've never been trained to listen. Perhaps our upbringing is such that no one has listened to us so why should we listen to them?

Here are some of the things that prevent us from listening?

- Physical tiredness or discomfort
  We may be tired or hungry. We may be hot or cold. We may be under stress and feel anxious or unwell.

- Distractions and mind wandering
  We may be distracted because of a noise. Or we may be thinking ahead of all the things that need to be done. We may be worried about someone or something.

- Reactions to the speaker
  We may dislike the person who is talking to us. We may find them boring or opinionated.

So how can we improve our listening skills?

○ Start listening with the first word and then listen intently

○ Stop what you are doing and listen – don't be tempted to do two things at once

○ Turn off all negative thoughts you have about the speaker

○ Think at the speed they're talking, don't jump ahead

○ Do not interrupt

○ Judge the content and not the delivery

○ Suspend your judgment and keep an open mind

○ Resist distractions if you possibly can

○ Make listening noises; particularly if you are on the telephone, and if face-to-face ensure that your body language conveys attentiveness, and give good eye contact.

In summary

○ listening is an essential part of being a good communicator

○ listening involves:

- the ability to understand what is being said

- the ability to organize and analyze the messages in order to retain them for subsequent use.

○ there are two types of listening:

1. Casual listening

2. Critical listening

○ casual listening is what we tend to do most of the time, we are only half listening

○ critical listening requires concentration and stamina

○ there are many things that prevent us from listening. These include:

- Mental laziness

- Different perspectives

- Strong emotions

- Physical tiredness or discomfort

- Desire to talk

- Distractions and mind wandering

- Reactions to the speaker

Chapter 7

Assertiveness

In order to provide exceptional customer service you need to employ staff who can behave assertively. We are not born assertive: it is something that we need to learn.

Human beings are primed to behave in a certain way when faced with danger, or when threatened. Our natural reflexes mean that we will either want to run away from danger, or attack whoever is causing it before it gets us. This is known as the flight or fight response and can be translated into us either behaving submissively (flight) or behaving aggressively (fight).

In today's society however it is not acceptable that we behave in this manner. If we do then we could end up in trouble with the law. It certainly isn't acceptable behaviour when dealing with customers. Furthermore, behaving aggressively is bad for your health resulting in an increased heart rate, which can lead to high blood pressure, and therefore the possibility of heart attack and strokes. And behaving submissively leads to low self worth and a lack of confidence, which in turn can result in greater exposure to viruses, infections and depression.

Behaving assertively therefore benefits us as individuals and also benefits our customers.

What does assertiveness mean?

An assertive person has the confidence to express opinions whilst respecting the rights of others. It is someone who is keen to reach solutions to conflicts that give satisfaction to both sides. An assertive person will listen to the customer and will not impose their views on him/her. They will however stand their ground if they need to in a non-threatening manner. Their body language is confident and open, and their eye contact good.

An assertive person has:

- a positive attitude
- an open mind about people
- good self esteem and confidence
- is approachable

Assertive behaviour also enables us to deal with difficult people and situations more confidently.

Before we examine how to behave assertively towards customers let's just take a closer look at submissive and aggressive behaviour.

What does submissive behaviour mean?

Submissive behaviour means neglecting to defend your personal rights and beliefs. You put the rights of others before your own rights. You constantly give in when you shouldn't and then feel very upset about it. You find it difficult to communicate with awkward and demanding customers. You back down in situations where you should have stood your ground. You may also find yourself blaming others for mistakes that you have made, or blaming the company policy. You refuse to take calls in case they might be from demanding customers and you make promises that you can't keep just to get the customer off your back and then leave your colleagues to clear up the mess!

What makes us become submissive?

We can become submissive when we are under attack or even when we think we are going to be attacked. If confronted by an angry, over confident or demanding customer we cannot afford to run away, or simply capitulate. We need to handle him/her in an assertive, confident manner. This is not always easy and some techniques are provided in this book in chapter eight to help you do this.

What does aggressive behaviour mean?

Aggressive behaviour means that you consider your rights and beliefs are more important than the other person and you say so. Alternatively you could behave in an underhand and manipulative manner to get your own way. You refuse to let the customer finish explaining what it is he wants, or what the problem is. You interrupt him and look exasperated, or hostile. Your body language is closed. Your voice is terse and abrupt. You might resort to using put downs, for example, 'Well what did you expect for the money!'

What makes us become aggressive?

People often adopt aggressive behaviour because it gets them what they want. It can also give them a sense of power, and sometimes it covers up for their own insecurity.

So let's now examine how we should behave assertively towards our customers

Having an open mind – developing a positive inner voice

I have already mentioned the importance of having a positive inner voice and now I want to look at this in more detail. Getting the right inner voice can help you to become more assertive and therefore handle those difficult situations and people more confidently. Here is an example to illustrate this.

Example

A customer who is continually complaining about your organization's services is coming towards you. He is very difficult and demanding and you find dealing with him tough.

This might be the dialogue that is going on inside your head:

> 'Oh, no, not him again! Why do I always get to deal with him? He's a real nuisance, a nightmare. He's always complaining. He's no right to behave like this to me. Who does he think he is?'

Your feelings are of frustration, anger, and impatience. If you don't correct this negative inner voice your behaviour will reflect those feelings and you will behave aggressively towards this customer. This will show in your body language and expression, and in your choice of words and your tone of voice. The customer will pick up on this behaviour and react in an even more aggressive manner; you clash and have a no win situation.

And what if your inner dialogue is something like this?

> 'Oh, no, not him again! Why does he always pick on me? Nothing I do is ever right. I find him so difficult to deal with. I know he'll shout and bawl at me and walk all over me. Help!'

Here you are going to end up being submissive, giving in to this man's every whim, letting him walk all over you – not very good for either you or the organization.

So how should you change this to a more assertive response?

First recognise that your inner voice is wrong. It is negative in both the above scenarios. It is aggressive and defensive.

Once you do this you then have the opportunity to change it to a more positive inner voice – something along the lines of:

> 'It's Mr Brown again. I know he is a difficult person to deal with, but I can handle him. I can keep calm, listen to what he has to say, and deal with his queries and demands in a competent and professional manner. I am in control of the situation and myself.'

I don't promise it will be easy at first, it takes a bit of practice, but with this kind of dialogue going through your head, your body language and posture will be more positive and you will project a more confident image, which in turn will communicate itself to the customer.

Keep your body posture upright and hold eye contact without glaring at the customer. If you drop your eye contact you automatically go into submissive mode. Try to use the customer's name, it helps to build rapport and shows respect.

There are more techniques on dealing with difficult and angry customers in chapter eight, but a positive inner voice is the first step to handling this successfully.

You can't win over everyone but you can deal with them in a professional manner. Everyone has a point of view it doesn't have to be the same as yours. In fact life would be pretty boring if it was. We are all individual personalities, with different upbringing and experiences, which influence the way we communicate. Keep an open mind and seek first to understand and then be understood and you won't go far wrong. (For more information on assertiveness read *Being Positive and Staying Positive even when the going gets tough*).

And remember the old proverb **Practice makes Perfect**.

In summary

○ there are three main types of behaviour:

> Assertive
> Aggressive
> Submissive

○ submissive means neglecting to defend your personal rights and beliefs

○ aggressive means considering your rights and beliefs are more important than other people's

○ assertive means standing up for your own rights without violating the rights of others

○ being assertive means that you are confident enough to express your opinions, views and ideas and to deal with customers in a professional manner

○ people behave aggressively because it gives them a sense of power and sometimes it covers up for their own insecurity

○ people behave aggressively if they are threatened

❍ people become submissive when they are under attack or when they think they are going to be attacked

❍ submissive individuals usually have low self esteem

❍ when dealing with customers make sure your inner voice is positive

Chapter 8

Dealing with the angry or difficult person

Dealing with angry people is never easy. You need to learn how to express yourself without losing your temper or bursting into tears. In the previous chapter I started to examine how you can deal with difficult people by getting the right inner voice. Aggressive people can come at us out of the blue when we are least prepared for them. The attack can cause us to go into fight or flight mode i.e. to become aggressive or submissive before we are even fully aware this is what we are doing. We need to find a response to these situations that leaves us feeling neither cross nor upset and the customer satisfied with the outcome of the exchange.

The technique I examine below is appropriate for dealing with that angry or complaining person both face-to-face and on the telephone.

Generally speaking people are usually braver on the telephone than they are face-to-face because the visual element is missing so the anger may be more intense. The compensating factor here though is that at least they can't attack you physically!

In order to deal with the angry customer you need to understand the three stages of anger.

Three stages of anger

Stage 1

When someone comes at you angrily they are usually ranting and raving. This can be very upsetting because it feels like a personal onslaught. It isn't. It is important to tell yourself that the customer isn't angry with you, personally, but at something that your organization has done (albeit possibly by a member of staff) to annoy that customer.

> **The customer is angry at the situation, not you.**

Perhaps your organization has failed to deliver what was promised. Perhaps someone has sent the customer the wrong piece of equipment. Maybe a promised call back hasn't materialised. Whatever the reason, your task is to try and resolve the problem. If you don't successfully resolve it at this stage it will escalate to stage two.

STAGE 2

Now the anger becomes directed at you personally. This is where you may get abusive language and threats.

STAGE 3

The third level of anger is where it becomes directed at everyone else. This may not sound very harmful, but believe me it could ruin your organization's reputation.

At this stage of anger the customer is threatening to call the newspapers, contact a consumer affairs programme, take your organization to court, and generally tell everyone how useless your company is. Bad news travels fast and your sales could be seriously affected.

**Anger needs to be resolved at Stage 1
when it is directed at the situation
and not you personally.**

By the time people complain they have usually worked themselves up into a state. This isn't only because they feel angry, but it can also be because they are extremely nervous. Perhaps they don't know how to complain. They may be afraid of being ridiculed, or perhaps they don't have the vocabulary to be able to express themselves clearly, and explain how they feel. This means that by the time they call you on the telephone, or come storming into your office or shop, they are ready to let rip.

Handling the angry customer

Here is how you should handle the situation:

1. Get the right inner voice – tell yourself that you can handle this; you can keep calm. The customer is not angry at you but at something that has happened. You need to help resolve this to your and the customer's satisfaction.

2. Get the right body language. If you are face-to-face with the customer then keep your body posture upright, but not stiff or aggressive, and hold eye contact as best you can. Some people won't look at you when they are very angry; instead their eye contact is roving all over the place. Alternatively, some angry people may be glaring at you and it can be very intimidating holding their eye contact.

3. Listen actively. Don't let your mind get distracted by thinking negative thoughts about the other person. Make listening noises to show that you are listening, particularly on the telephone, for example: uh huh, yes. If face-to-face then occasionally nod to show you are listening.

4. Do not try to interrupt them or reason with them. You can never begin to reason with someone who is angry or upset until they have worked their anger out. Let them get it off their chest. They need to have their say. Eventually they will run out of steam. They will have to pause if only to take a breath. It is only after this that you can move onto the next stage. If you need to isolate the customer from the public area then trying to do so whilst they are in full flow is disastrous. It will only fuel their anger, as will interrupting them and trying to reason with them. Unfortunately if someone does erupt in a public area, you just have to adopt the above techniques and put up with it. It is not pleasant but it will pass if handled correctly, and you will be able to resolve whatever is upsetting the customer.

5. Re state/summarize the situation. Now that the customer has had his say you have the opportunity to speak. For example, *'Let me check I've understood, Mr. Jones. We promised you delivery of this equipment on Tuesday and you've still not received it, is that correct?'* The customer now knows that you have listened and summarized the problem correctly. If you haven't, or if you have misunderstood the problem, this allows the customer the opportunity of correcting you. If you can use the customer's name in conversation this also helps you to build rapport.

6. Ask open questions. If you are not in a position to summarize from what the customer has said, then you may need to ask him or her **open questions** to probe deeper, to find out exactly what the problem is. Alternatively you may need to ask further **open questions** to correctly resolve the problem.

Open questions begin with:

> Who
> What
> Where
> When
> How
> Why

Open questions will give you information. They are designed to:

○ Help you properly understand what it is the customer wants.

○ Help the customer feel important.

○ Help you find out how the customer feels about you and your organization

○ Help you control the conversation.

For example:
'When did we promise you delivery?'

'Who did you speak to about this?'

'How many items did you receive?'

There are further types of questions that could help you handle the awkward or difficult situation. Here are some of them.

Exploratory questions, which are also open questions
'What happened after that?'

'What do you mean by that?'

Clarifying the situation and summarizing

'Let me just make sure I've understood this, Mr Smith. What you're saying is…'

'I'm not sure I understand, Mrs Jones, could you clarify that for me please?'

Interpreting

'Are you perhaps saying…'

Supportive

'Go on, please.'

Encouraging the customer and reassuring him.

Empathic

'It sounds as though…'

'I can see that you're obviously very upset about this.'

'I understand, Mr Jones, and I would be angry with that if it happened to me. Now let me see how I can resolve this for you.'

Reflective

Repeating statements made in a reflective way.

Self-disclosing

Sharing your own experiences about a particular issue.

> 'That happened to me once and I completely understand how you must feel. Now let me see how I can resolve this for you.'

It is at this stage that you may wish to isolate the customer from the public area. After restating the problem you might wish to say something along the lines of:

> 'Let's take a seat in the interview room, Mr. Jones and then I can resolve this situation for you.'

By now the customer's anger will have subsided and he or she will be ready to answer your questions and accompany you to a private area.

Beneficial Intent Statement

In the example above I have used what is called the **beneficial intent statement** i.e. 'Let's take a seat in the interview room, Mr. Jones and let me see **how I can resolve this situation for you.'** This strengthens the bond between you and the customer.

If you have taken an angry telephone call, and need to ask the customer to wait whilst you check something, then be lavish in explaining what you are doing, especially if it involves a silence while the caller 'hangs on'. Remember he can't see you, and he will interpret any silence as inactivity. If you need to put the customer on hold then ensure him that you will get back to him promptly, or offer to ring him back, and tell him when that will be. Don't say, 'I'll call you back later.' This is too vague. Later to you might mean tomorrow morning when the customer is expecting a call within the next thirty minutes. If the customer has to call your organization again, he will be VERY ANGRY, especially if he has to explain the problem all over again, and to someone else. Take ownership of the problem. For example: 'I will call you back in twenty minutes' and THEN DO SO, even if you are still trying to track down an answer. Telling the customer that you are still 'on the case' will make him much happier.

This kind of follow up can often be difficult for some organizations that operate call centres where staff are working on different shifts. It is often one of the reasons why call centres get a bad press. It is no excuse. A call centre must find ways of operating in an efficient manner by putting the customer's needs first. After all no customers no organization!

7. Resolve it. Now you need to tell the customer how you are going to resolve the situation for him i.e. what you are going to do about his complaint. Another technique is to ask the customer what he would like you to do, thereby putting the ball in his court. For example, 'How might I resolve this for you, Mr Smith?' Or 'What would you like me to do, Mr Smith?'

8. Then do it. Take action. Don't promise to resolve something and then do nothing about it.

9. Follow up. Check that any action promised has been carried out even if wasn't your responsibility to do so. If you took the complaint, you must take responsibility for seeing it through to a satisfactory conclusion.

As a final gesture telephone the customer and check that the situation has been resolved to his satisfaction. This final touch often turns what was a potentially disastrous customer relation's exercise into a good one, and you may have won a customer for life if handled professionally and efficiently.

10. Then ask, what would have prevented this problem? What changes do you need to make to ensure it doesn't happen again? An organization that continually allows mistakes to happen and doesn't deliver its promises isn't going to be around for very long.

Checklist for handling difficult/angry customers

DON'T

☐   Interrupt
☐   Be patronising
☐   Jump to conclusions
☐   Argue
☐   Lose your temper
☐   Blame others.

DO

☐   Shut up and listen
☐   Use the customer's name
☐   Take notes – but not too many if face-to-face, remember to keep that eye contact
☐   Let the customer make his case
☐   Ask questions to clarify the details
☐   Confirm with the customer that you understand the nature of the problem
☐   Tell the customer what you propose to do to put things right
☐   Make sure it is done
☐   Show empathy.

Handling the unreasonable and aggressive customer

But what if you're right and they are wrong?

If their grievance is unjustified i.e. they are in the wrong and you are in the right, or the customer won't calm down or be reasonable, then you need to adopt what is called the **consequence technique**. Here you should follow stages 1-5 as discussed in the previous section on dealing with the difficult customer i.e.

1. Get the right inner voice
2. Get the right body language
3. Listen actively
4. Don't interrupt or try to reason with them – let the customer have his head of steam
5. Restate/summarize

You may even get to the next stage and be able to ask some open questions to try and find out what is at the root of the problem. Or you may need to explain your company's procedure or policy that puts the customer in the wrong and you in the right. In this case you need to state where you stand but show you are still interested in the customer's opinions and feelings. For example:

> *'I recognise you have strong feelings on this, Mrs. Smith, but we see it differently.'*

Here you have also empathized to a degree by recognizing the customer's feelings but you have balanced this with stating your viewpoint. You may need to continue by adding something along the lines of:

> *'It is our policy not to allow smoking, (dogs) (children) because…'* and give a valid reason.

If the aggression is still maintained then you need to **step up** your assertiveness. Increase the emphasis on **your** position.

> 'It is our policy.'

If the aggression continues and the customer becomes abusive then you can use the **consequence technique.**

For example:

> 'If you continue to shout in this way, Mrs Smith, I will put the phone down and ring you back later when you have calmed down.'

Or

> 'If you continue to behave in this manner, Mrs Smith, then I must ask you to leave.'

If all your efforts have failed then cut off the interaction, you have warned them.

I have only had to resort to this once in my career when I was working in a busy inner city job centre. A customer became abusive. I warned him that if he continued to shout and swear at me I would refuse to deal with him. When he didn't stop I got up from my desk and walked away. I had a great boss who backed me up and told the man that until he learnt how to behave no one would deal with him.

Whatever the reason for anger do try to keep calm, get a positive inner voice and hold on to it. Try first to understand how the other person feels, where **they** are coming from, rather than focusing on how you feel.

In summary

O aggressive people can come at us out of the blue when we are least prepared for them.

O there are three stages of anger:

> **Stage 1** – The customer is angry at the situation, not you.
>
> **Stage 2** – The anger becomes directed at you personally.
>
> **Stage 3** – The customer is threatening to sue you or tell the newspapers

O anger needs to be resolved at Stage 1 when it is directed at the situation and not you personally

O by the time people complain they have usually worked themselves up into a state

O the way to handle anger is as follows:

> 1. Get the right inner voice
> 2. Get the right body language.
> 3. Listen actively.

4. Do not try to interrupt them or reason with them.
5. Re state/summarize the situation.
6. Ask open questions.
7. Say what you are going to do to resolve the problem
8. Then do it.
9. Follow up.
10. Ask what would have prevented this problem? What changes do we need to make to ensure it doesn't happen again?

❍ if the customer's grievance is unjustified step up your assertiveness

❍ if the customer becomes abusive, or refuses to calm down, adopt the consequence technique

❍ whatever the reason for anger do try to keep calm, get a positive inner voice and hold on to it

❍ try first to understand how the other person feels, where **they** are coming from, rather than focusing on how you feel.

Chapter 9

Professional telephone behaviour

Many customers are lost through poor telephone handling and couldn't-care-less attitudes. In this chapter I cover the fundamentals of good telephone practice. For more information on converting enquiries into orders and telemarketing, read *The Easy Step by Step Guide to Telemarketing, Cold Calling & Appointment Making*.

Because the telephone is a non-visual tool – the customer can't see you and you can't see them –
it is important that you use your voice in the most powerful and constructive way you can because the customer is making an initial judgment about your organization based on how you sound.

> **People will base their judgments on what you say, or rather what they think you say and how you say it!**

There are other problems associated with using the telephone when dealing with customers and potential customers.

○ It is **more difficult to establish rapport** on the telephone because the face-to-face visual element is missing.

○ The **telephone is intrusive** - you could be calling someone at an inconvenient time.

○ **People are more likely to jump more readily to wrong conclusions**. This is because people hear what they want to hear, or they could misinterpret your tone of voice. Likewise you could leap to the wrong conclusions about the customer based on how he or she sounds.

○ **Callers and customers are tempted to do other things whilst talking on the telephone, which will break concentration.** The customer might not be listening to you and you might not be giving the customer your full attention. Therefore vital information could be lost.

○ **It is more difficult to communicate accurate information** – people remember more of what they see than hear.

○ You can be cut off at any time. You may have a bad line, or you may have trouble understanding the customer's accent.

Good telephone practice therefore includes the following:

○ Answer the telephone promptly – within three to five rings. If it does have to ring longer make sure you apologize for keeping the caller waiting.

○ Start each call by saying who you are, your name, position or department.

○ Establish and use the other person's name early in the telephone conversation.

○ Ask open questions to find out what the caller requires. Open questions begin with: who, what, where, how, when and why. If the call is an enquiry regarding your services, or a request for a brochure then don't forget to ask how the customer heard of your organization. Take full details and read back the name and address. Ask the customer to spell his/her name.

○ Listen. Resist the temptation to interrupt.

○ When listening demonstrate you are listening by making listening noises such as 'Yes' 'Really' 'I see.'

○ Concentrate. Don't be tempted to do two things at once. Give the telephone conversation your undivided attention.

○ Make notes and read back key points so that the caller knows you are being attentive.

○ Be lavish in explaining what you are doing, especially if it involves a silence while the caller 'hangs on.'

○ Use assertive behaviour to control the call. Stay assertive even when you don't feel like it and especially when dealing with an aggressive or submissive person.

○ Finish by recapping exactly what it is you are going to do as a result of the telephone conversation.

○ Smile for, even though you can't be seen by the other person, if you smile it helps your voice to sound more assertive and friendly.

○ Record details of the call, make sure any action promised is carried out, and follow up if necessary.

How to establish and build rapport

Don't shout and don't talk too quietly.

If you shout down the line the customer will be put off by too loud a voice. Conversely if you are too quiet he/she will walk all over you. The voice must convey a great deal. The first few seconds are vital for the right impression: warm, friendly, alert and wanting to communicate effectively.

Matching the speed of their voice.

Mirror/pace your voice with the customer. For example, if the customer is slower speaking, then slow down. If you continue to talk at them like a babbling idiot, or fire questions at them, they will feel intimidated. Likewise, if you are dealing with a more direct individual, then be direct back.

Vary your pitch and make sure you do not sound droll.

The telephone drains thirty per cent of the energy level in your voice. Therefore you must make it sound more enthusiastic.

Avoid anger.

We all collect anger. Get rid of it in your voice – walk away, calm down before you pick up the telephone again because your emotions come through on the telephone. Likewise, if you are depressed then you will sound depressed.

Body posture.

Look and be alert. If your body is slouched your voice will sound slouched and couldn't-care-less. Imagine the other person sitting in front of you. How would you look then? Alert and interested, I hope. Keep your head up. This puts less pressure on your vocal chords. And if you want to sound more serious then keep your head and body still when you talk, this helps to invest your voice with more authority.

Body Language.

Use the same body language on the telephone as you would normally face-to-face. This enables the enthusiasm to come through in your voice. Stand up to take difficult calls; it gives your voice more authority.

Words and phrases to avoid

There are some words and phrases that really annoy customers.

Here are some of the more common ones.

Problem

If the customer is angry and you say to him or her 'What's the problem?' or even worse, 'What's your problem,' they are likely to reply, 'I haven't got a problem – it's your company that's got the problem.'

Complaint

Likewise the word 'complaint' invites people to make a complaint and also sounds as if they've got something wrong with them medically. Why not simply say 'Please tell me what happened?' or 'What's the situation?'

You *have* to

A very emotive phrase particularly if the customer is angry. He or she may well say, 'I don't *have* to do anything.' Instead you could say, 'Could I ask you to put that in writing, Mr. Jones?'

You must appreciate

This often sends customers screaming up the wall! I don't have to appreciate anything, particularly when it is done to suit your organization and not me, the customer! Why must I appreciate your problems? I am the customer. I am paying for this service or product.

There's nothing I can do

Always tell people what you **can** do – not what you can't do. Or simply say, 'Let me check on that and get back to you.' And, don't forget always tell them when you will get back to them.

He's out at the moment

By all means say if someone isn't available but then ask if anyone else can help, or if you can take a message. The number of times I have had to ask whether anyone else can help me is incredible. Always volunteer that extra bit of information or help.

'I apologize' sounds more assertive than 'I'm sorry.'

And if you hear staff using phrases like this about your customers then you need to revise your customer service policy:

> 'Tell the customer I'll ring him back later.'

> 'I'm going to lunch now I can't take that call.'

> 'It's not my fault. It's nothing to do with me.'

> 'I don't know where he is at the moment.'

> 'That customer is a blessed nuisance.'

> 'Oh it's Mrs. Smith, she's always complaining. Tell her I'm out.'

> 'I'm too busy to deal with that now.'

And to the customer...

> 'Could you ring back later, he's busy with an important customer at the moment.

No thank you!!

Speaking to improve communication

○ Tailor what you say to the understanding of the receiver and the level of knowledge he or she already has.

○ Explain jargon.

○ Be logical in the presentation of what you say – as would appear logical to the receiver.

○ Speak in manageable chunks. No one should be expected to listen attentively non-stop for more than about five minutes.

○ Invite comment and feedback, if not offered spontaneously.

If you need more help on how to communicate more effectively then you may like to read *Communicating with more Confidence* by Pauline Rowson.

In summary

○ many customers are lost through poor telephone handling and couldn't care less attitudes

○ people will base their judgments on what you say, or rather what they think you say and how you say it!

○ it is more difficult to establish rapport on the telephone, and people are more likely to jump more readily to wrong conclusions

○ don't be tempted to do other things whilst talking on the telephone; it will break your concentration

○ answer the telephone promptly and apologize if you have kept the customer waiting

○ introduce yourself clearly and slowly

○ jot down the customer's name as soon as he/she gives it and use it immediately in the next sentence

○ ask open questions to find out what the caller requires

○ check the spelling of the customer's name and read back details to make sure you have got the message correct

○ listen actively and make listening noises

○ be lavish in explaining what you are doing, especially if it involves a silence while the caller 'hangs on'

○ use assertive behaviour to control the call

○ smile. It helps your voice to sound more assertive and friendly

○ make sure any action promised is carried out

○ don't shout and don't talk too quietly

○ match the speed of their voice

○ vary your pitch and make sure you do not sound droll

○ avoid anger

○ look and be alert. Keep your head up

○ use the same body language on the telephone as you would normally face-to-face

○ stand up to take difficult calls; it gives your voice more authority

○ try not to use the word 'problem

○ always tell people what you can do – not what you can't do

○ always volunteer that extra bit of information or help

○ 'I apologize' sounds more assertive than 'I'm sorry'

○ tailor what you say to the understanding of the receiver and the level of knowledge he or she already has

○ explain jargon and speak in manageable chunks

○ invite comment and feedback, if not offered spontaneously.

Chapter 10

Going the extra mile

It's not just about meeting your customers' expectations but exceeding them. By doing this you can win more business.

Take time to communicate with your customers on a regular basis in the manner that they prefer. This could be by e mail, telephone, letter, newsletter, in person, and in some businesses by inviting them to a corporate hospitality event.

Collect information on your customers and their buying habits and patterns and use this to communicate with them in the most effective way, tailoring promotional offers to suit them, or providing them with new information about products or services.

Telephone customers on a regular basis to check they are happy with your products and services and introduce new services and products if appropriate.

If appropriate to your business ensure you have the right account managers calling on your existing customers and checking they are satisfied with your organization's services. Don't let them just be order takers. Their job is to sell more to your customers by offering them solutions to their problems, or by satisfying a need. (For more information on this see *The Easy Step by Step Guide to Successful Selling*).

Undertake marketing initiatives that benefit your local community, for example become involved in charitable donations or fundraising events.

Your staff may wish to work with voluntary organizations, or on projects in the community, which not only help develop them as individuals but also enriches the local community. Getting a group of staff to work on a charitable project in the community is also a great team building exercise.

Look at operating environmentally and eco friendly policies.

And finally…

Take care of your staff and they will take care of your customers.

For more information on all our books
visit www.rowmark.co.uk

For special sponsored and corporate
editions contact:
enquiries@rowmark.co.uk

Easy Step by Step Guides

from **ROWMARK**

- Quick and easy to read - from cover to cover in two hours
- Contain a handy bullet point summary at the end of each chapter
- Provide lots of tips and techniques
- Have a simple style and layout – making the books easy to read
- Jargon free – straightforward and easy to understand
- Strong branding – making it easy for readers to find and collect the titles
- Written by practitioners - people with real experience and who are 'experts' in their subject

Sales and Marketing

0953298760	Marketing £11.99	
0953298744	Successful Selling £9.99	
0953985628	Building a Positive Media Profile £9.99	
0953985636	Writing Advertising Copy £9.99	
0953985644	Writing Newsletters & Articles £9.99	
0953298752	Telemarketing, Cold Calling & Appointment Making £9.99	

Management

095398561X	Recruiting the Right Staff £9.99
0953985679	Giving Confident Presentations £9.99
0953298779	Motivating Staff for Better Performance £11.99
0953985652	Handling Confrontation £9.99
0953985601	Managing Change £9.99
0953985687	Fewer, Shorter, Better Meetings £9.99
0953298787	Better Budgeting for your Business £9.99

Personal Development

0953298736	Stress and Time Management £9.99 (New price)
0953985660	Being Positive & Staying Positive £9.99
0953985695	Communicating with More Confidence £9.99

Schools

095480452X	Fundraising for Your school £9.99

Essential business books and guides to help you and your organisation succeed